# Garden Prayers

For Diana, my wife,
who taught me the joy
of a garden prayer.

The publishing team included Carl Koch, development editor; Laurie Berg Rohda, manuscript editor; Barbara Bartelson, typesetter; Maurine Twait, art director; Elaine Kohner, illustrator; Tom Lowes, cover designer; front cover photo by Wayne Simsic; back cover photo by PhotoDisc, Inc.; pre-press, printing, and binding by the graphics division of Saint Mary's Press.

The acknowledgments continue on page 92.

Printed in the United States of America

Printing: 9 8 7 6 5 4 3 2 1

Year: 2004 03 02 01 00 99 98 97 96 95

ISBN 0-88489-360-X

Genuine recycled paper with 10% post-consumer waste. Printed with soy-based ink.

# Garden Prayers

## Planting the Seeds of Your Inner Life

Wayne Simsic

Saint Mary's Press
Christian Brothers Publications
Winona, Minnesota

# Contents

# Introduction

From the time I was a child, garden images nourished me and deepened my awareness of myself and the natural world. While hoeing seemingly endless rows of vegetables in the family garden, I attended the mystery of growth almost daily. Plucking large fleshy tomatoes in the hot sun, I discovered sweet reward for all the toil. Simple lessons, cultivating and harvesting, but they serve me well even today as I look out the window dreaming about potential gardens around a house into which my wife and I have recently settled.

Connection with gardens, even the smallest gardens, can become windows to our inner life. For a long time I have wanted to write a book about the intimate link between gardening and spirituality—a book of prayers actually, because gardening inspires the soul. Weeding and cultivating, planting and harvesting, celebrating successes and bemoaning failures teach us more about ourselves than we could imagine. May Sarton declared:

> Making a garden is not a gentle hobby for the elderly, to be picked up and laid down like a game of solitaire. It is a grand passion. It seizes a person whole, and once it has done so he will have to accept that his life is going to be radically changed. (*Plant Dreaming Deep*)

However, you don't have to be a dedicated gardener to discover the power of garden images for your inner life. You don't need to cultivate roses to realize that the rose is a profound and ancient symbol for love.

Experimenting a little helps tremendously. Plant seeds, any seeds, and watch them grow. Let your relationship with growing things become more personal as you observe the changes in a plant. Water it, watch it blossom, nourish it, draw it. Most important: pay attention and let the color of a particular plant become music for you. Let its form fill your imagination. Identify with it from within; do not be content with a name.

Garden images abound in the Scriptures as well as in the writings of saints and mystics throughout the centuries. There is a reason for this. Deep in our soul we know that we cultivate an inner garden of great importance. Within this garden we discover what it means to be more truly human and to love one another. We also become more aware of a secret hunger for infinite love that calls forth both wonder and fear: wonder at the overwhelming mystery of love, and fear that we will be transformed by it.

When all is said and done, gardeners are dreamers who seek Eden. They hope that a plot of land, properly cared for, will reap great rewards and become a center of harmony in the middle of daily struggles. Many gardeners vaguely realize, too, that they are involved in a spiritual enterprise. Binding themselves to soil, seed, and growth, they uncover the soul's own hidden process and engage a mysterious rhythm. The success of the garden is less important than the renewal of life—this is the primary source of delight.

This book of prayers was written for all who find garden images alive in their heart. The time has come to attend to these images, to harvest them. The prayers that follow have evolved from an experience of the earthy, sensuous garden that we struggle to cultivate and tame, as well as the garden of the heart where dreams and unconscious yearnings for happiness, peace, and harmony are uncovered. For anyone who truly loves a garden, can soul-work be far behind? "What an appealing image," writes Teresa of Ávila, "to think of my soul as a garden and imagine that the Lord was taking a walk in it" (adapted from *Collected Works*).

## Prayer Suggestions

1. I encourage you to spend time in a garden (any plot of ground or landscape that gives you a sense of "garden") for your prayer. Saints, mystics, and artists through the centuries have retreated to gardens of every kind, tame and wild.

If you pray in a garden, begin by exploring. Take as much time as you need to immerse yourself in the atmosphere. Really look at your surroundings—the signs of growth, the signs of decay. Open your senses to smells and sounds. Walk, bend down, and touch a cluster of thyme. Smell. Pick a sprig from a lavender bush and crush it between your fingers; rub the oil on your neck.

Walk a little further, find a place to sit, perhaps under an old, statuesque maple. Look up at the dense leaves as they shift softly in the light. Relax in the silence of the landscape. Listen to the silence at the center of your heart.

Read one of the prayers slowly and let the images and words ground you in your heart of hearts. Follow the path of your deepest desire and pray according to your own need for words or silence. Conclude with a short period of silence.

**2.** If your prayer does not take place outdoors, you can enter the garden through your imagination. Find a quiet place (perhaps you can look out a window at a garden, or sit in front of your favorite painting of a garden scene, or ponder a potted herb garden or special house plant) and spend some time relaxing. The more relaxed you are, physically and mentally, the more open you will be to the prayer experience.

Imagine a garden you would want to spend time in. Don't restrict your image. Let the garden take any form that appeals to you: country garden, formal garden, tropical garden, herb and vegetable garden, or garden by the sea. Then use your senses to place yourself in the garden. Imagine walking through the gate, picking up something from the ground, and holding it in your hand. Smell the air, any scents? What does the sky look like? Do some sense experiences seem more provocative than others?

Rest in this garden and allow it to be present to you. Does it represent any past garden places in your life? Try to listen to what this garden tells you about times of sadness and joy.

Slowly read one or more of the prayers. Let the words draw you into the garden of your heart. Find rest and nourishment inside this garden. Let it speak to your heart. Conclude with a short period of silence.

Let us now explore the garden with hands open and empty, extended toward the Creator. Nothing hurries you, nobody sets your pace. Let your prayer be simple, say the words as if you were saying them for the first time.

# The Gardener

## Opening

O Holy One,
may I always be the kind of gardener
who learns from gardens;
who is optimistic and hopeful,
who plans for, believes in,
and trusts in the future,
who realizes my proper place in nature
and my radical dependency on you
for all things,
especially the gift
of my own life.

## Reading

The Creator planted a garden in Eden, which is in
the east, and there put the human being fashioned
in the divine image.

(Adapted from Genesis 2:8)

## Reflection

All the accomplished gardeners I know are sur-
prisingly comfortable with failure. They may not
be happy about it, but instead of reacting with
anger or frustration, they seem freshly intrigued
by the peony that, after years of being taken for
granted, suddenly fails to bloom. They understand
that, in the garden at least, failure speaks louder
than success. By that I don't mean the gardener
encounters *more* failure than success (though in
some years he will), only that his failures have

more to say to him. . . . Outright success is
dumb, disaster frequently eloquent. At least to
the gardener who learns how to listen.

(Michael Pollan, *Second Nature*)

## Hymn

Sowing the seed,
my hand is one with the earth.

Wanting the seed to grow,
my mind is one with the light.

Hoeing the crop,
my hands are one with the rain.

Having cared for the plants,
my mind is one with the air.

Hungry and trusting,
my mind is one with the earth.

Eating the fruit,
my body is one with the earth.

(Wendell Berry, *Farming: A Handbook*)

## Closing

God, thank you
for the succession of gardens in my life,
those miniature paradises that have brought me
back down to earth.
Thank you for my longing for beauty
and the wisdom gained through failure,
but mostly,
thank you
for the wisdom
to follow my deepest desire.

# *Through the Gate*

## Opening

O gentle gatekeeper

. . . . . . .

You are the gardener,
and once you have opened the gate of the
   heavenly garden,
paradise,
you offer us the flowers
and the fruits
of the eternal Godhead.

(Catherine of Siena, Prayers)

## Reading

Open for me the gates of saving justice,
I shall go in and thank Yahweh.
This is the gate of Yahweh,
where the upright go in.
I thank you for hearing me,
and making yourself my Saviour.

(Psalm 118:19–21)

## Reflection

As a potent symbol in the history of religions, a
gate serves as a passageway from external reality to
the inner life. Entering a garden through a gate
is not a casual matter. It represents a change of
vision. Something radically new will be expected
from us. Ordinary matters that were once important give way to deeper values like self-surrender

and love. We become certain that our existence is meaningful and that life has a purpose. What a wide gate of grace the garden entrance becomes!

## Hymn

The one
essential
thing
is
that
we
open
the gate
to
a self
worthy
of all
our love.

## Closing

God, my friend, guide me
as I enter the gate
that leads to a deeper sense
of self.
Show me how to answer
the urgent longing
to receive your love
and find true wisdom.

# Morning Watch

## Opening

I am immersed in the silence of the garden
before the rising dawn.
Awaken my soul, God of all goodness,
so that I can praise you.

## Reading

Awake, my soul
awake, lyre and harp,
I mean to wake the dawn!
I mean to thank you among the peoples,
to sing your praise among the nations.
Your love reaches to the heavens,
your faithfulness to the clouds.
Rise high above the heavens, God,
let your glory cover the earth!

(Psalm 57:8–11)

## Reflection

Walking in the morning garden before anyone is
awake, wrapped against the chill dawn air, I watch
the shadows fly away and the light break. The
morning especially holds an extraordinary silence.
The earth seems to revolve on a point of calm,
and the silence is so alive you can feel it among
the trees, weaving through the vegetation and the
shadows. There is no sense of separation, only the
shadows collecting and then disappearing with

the light, the soft breeze smelling like perfume,
and my eyes wide with compassion for the unveil-
ing of so much that is fresh and new.

## Hymn

O joys! Infinite sweetness! with what flowers,
And shoots of glory, my soul breaks and buds!

. . . . . . . . . . . . .

    The rising winds,
    And falling springs,
    Birds, beasts, all things
  Adore him in their kinds.
    Thus all is hurled
In sacred *hymns,* and *order,* the great *chime*
And *symphony* of nature. Prayer is
    The world in tune,
    A spirit-voice,
    And vocal joys
  whose *echo* is heaven's bliss.
           (Henry Vaughan, "Morning-Watch")

## Closing

Let me join my prayer
with all nature
toward you, loving Creator.
The world is music
and the morning rises
with hymns of praise.

# Garden of Dreams

## Opening

All would be well, Blessed One,
if I could
live
in the garden of my dreams,
like a child,
and celebrate the innocent and joyful
music
of the soul.

## Reading

But Jesus called the children to him and said, "Let
the little children come to me, and do not stop
them; for it is to such as these that the kingdom of
God belongs. In truth I tell you, anyone who does
not welcome the kingdom of God like a little
child will never enter it."

(Luke 18:16–17)

## Reflection

"Come with me and I'll show you," she said.

She led him round the laurel path and to the
walk where the ivy grew so thickly. Dickon fol-
lowed her with a queer, almost pitying, look on
his face. He felt as if he were being led to look at
some strange bird's nest and must move softly.
When she stepped to the wall and lifted the hang-
ing ivy he started. There was a door and Mary
pushed it slowly open and they passed in together,

and then Mary stood and waved her hand round
defiantly.

"It's this," she said. "It's a secret garden, and
I'm the only one in the world who wants it to be
alive."

(Frances Burnett, *The Secret Garden*)

## Hymn

It's the country of childhood
authentic fairyland—walled garden
silent under cypresses
wild violets, primroses awake
in a delicate wood, stone bridge
spanning the legendary stream
marble pillars, dim heraldic halls.
I am the child of exiles who dreamt
of the lost garden.

(Lauris Edmond, "Jardin des Colombières")

## Closing

God, my courteous guide,
lead me into the mysterious garden
where I can find refuge
and freely explore
the deepest dreams and hopes
that shape my life.
Forgive me for forgetting
an innocent faith
and allowing worries to consume
my heart.
Teach me to trust
the childlike voice that directs
my life.

# Tending the Garden

## Opening

God, you who give strength for every task,
I buy the equipment,
receive mail-order catalogs,
prepare the soil, plant,
and then allow the garden
to revert to weeds and disease.
Help me
keep the passion for my work,
even in barren times,
so that it does not return to chaos.

## Reading

I passed by a lazy person's field.
The gardener had no sense of how to tend a
   vineyard.
Thorns sprang up everywhere,
and weeds grew in rank profusion.
The stone wall had crumbled.
On the other hand, those who work their land
will have an abundance of bread.
The gardener who just fantasizes
will have only fantasies to eat.
        (Adapted from Proverbs 24:30–32; 12:11)

## Reflection

Beginners must realize that in order to give delight
to the Lord they are starting to cultivate a garden
on very barren soil, full of weeds. God pulls up

weeds and plants good seed. . . . And with the help of God we must work like good gardeners to get these plants to grow and take care to water them so that they don't wither but come to bud and flower. . . . Then God will often come to take pleasure in this garden.

(Adapted from Teresa of Ávila, *Collected Works*)

## Hymn

I saw a gardener
digging, digging, and sweating,
turning the soil over and over,
watering the plants at the proper time.
He persevered in his work,
and caused streams to run,
and abundant fruit to grow,
which he brought before God
and offered it
as thanksgiving.

(Adapted from Julian of Norwich, *Showings*)

## Closing

Let me apply the energy of my heart to this work,
God, you who are the source of life,
though the task is often laborious
and the results not immediately evident.
As I bend my knee to the earth,
I bend my heart to you as well.
Let me make this slow work a labor of love.

# Gardener's Year

## Opening

Let me find diversity and delight
in the changing seasons,
God of all creation.
As nature's drama unfolds
I reflect on the seasons of my life
and answer the cycles outside
with a deepening sensitivity
to the changes within.

## Reading

As long as earth endures:
seed-time and harvest,
cold and heat,
summer and winter,
day and night
will never cease.

(Genesis 8:22)

I shall give you the rain you need at the right time;
the soil will yield its produce and the trees of the
countryside their fruit; you will thresh until vin-
tage time and gather grapes until sowing time. You
will eat your fill of bread and live secure in your
land.

(Leviticus 26:4–5)

## Reflection

After weeks of frost and the fields brown and the
harvest long taken and the garden ripped up and

dumped and the trees mostly bare and the house tucked up for Winter—comes the moment of miraculous restoration, Summer's curtain call or triumphal final tour: The wind relents, the sun rises, golden warmth risen from frozen acres. . . . Late asters and chrysanthemums hover in summery air along with other late survivors: maybe the spindly autumnal goldenrod. Soon, sure enough, frost will blacken Fall's flowers and snow tamp them down with its orgy of sensuous deprivation, but now for five days or seven they float a warm raft of mid-Summer on the lake of Fall's desolation.

(Donald Hall, *Seasons at Eagle Pond*)

## Hymn

Silly gardener! summer goes,
And winter comes with pinching toes,
When in the garden bare and brown
You must lay your barrow down.

Well now, and while the summer stays
To profit by these garden days
O how much wiser you would be

.   .   .   .   .   .   .   .   .   .   .

(Robert Louis Stevenson, "The Gardener")

## Closing

God of seasons,
guide me through the rhythms of my life,
through life and death,
abundance and scarcity, light and dark.
Keep me protected in the palm of your hand;
calm my troubled heart.
I long for spring after winter's death.

# The Passage of Time

## Opening

God of life and death,
I cut grass,
rake fallen leaves,
prepare the garden for winter sleep.
As the days
get shorter
and colder
my mood is winter,
focused on the passage of life
and signs of death.

## Reading

Yahweh, you have been my security
from generation after generation.

. . . . . . . . . . . . .

A thousand years are like yesterday to you—
come and gone—
no more than a moment in the night.
You sweep humans away like daydreams,
like fresh grass which springs up
and flowers in the morning,
but by evening is withered and dry.

(Psalm 90:1–5)

## Reflection

The grandeurs of life are like the flowers in color
and in fate; the beauty of these remains so long as
their chaste buds gather and store the rich pearls
of the dawn and saving it, drop it in liquid dew;

but scarcely has the Cause of All directed upon
them the full rays of the sun, when their beauty
and glory fail, and the brilliant gay colors which
decked forth their pride wither and fade.

The delicious realms of flowers count their
dynasties by short periods; those which in the
morning revel proudly in beauty and strength,
by evening weep for the sad destruction of their
thrones. . . .

All things of earth have an end, and in the
midst of the most joyous lives, the breath falters,
they fall, they sink into the ground.

(Aztec, "Song of Nezahualcoyotl")

## Hymn

Farewell dear flowers, sweetly your time ye spent,
Fit, while ye lived, for smell or ornament,
    And after death for cures.
I follow straight without complaints or grief,
Since if my scent be good, I care not, if
    It be as short as yours.

(George Herbert, "Life")

## Closing

God of wisdom,
teach me to order my days
in the right way,
give priority
to the things most important,
make better use of my hours.
When the morning breaks,
let me depend even more on your love
and find shelter in you
even when I face times of hopelessness.

# Planting Seeds

## Opening

Creator of all that grows from seed,
light of all who are in darkness,
awaken me to the miracle of growth
—roots, leaves, blossoms—
the possibilities of my life in you.

## Reading

This is what the Reign of God will be like.
Gardeners spread seed on the soil.
At night while they are sleeping,
and during the day while they are awake,
the seeds sprout and grow.
How?
They do not know.

(Adapted from Mark 4:26–27)

This is the Spirit that is in my heart, smaller than
a grain of rice, or a grain of barley, or a grain of
mustard-seed, or a grain of canary-seed, or the
kernel of a grain of canary-seed. This is the Spirit
that is in my heart, greater than the earth, greater
than the sky, greater than heaven itself, greater
than all these worlds.

(Juan Mascaró, trans., The Upanishads)

## Reflection

Every moment and every event of every man's life
on earth plants something in his soul. For just as

the wind carries thousands of winged seeds, so each moment brings with it germs of spiritual vitality that come to rest imperceptibly in the minds and wills of men. Most of these unnumbered seeds perish and are lost, because men are not prepared to receive them: for such seeds as these cannot spring up anywhere except in the good soil of freedom, spontaneity and love.

(Thomas Merton, *New Seeds of Contemplation*)

## Hymn

I can hear, underground, that sucking and sobbing,
In my veins, in my bones I feel it,—
The small waters seeping upward,
The tight grains parting at last.
When sprouts break out,
Slippery as fish,
I quail, lean to beginnings, sheath-wet.

(Theodore Roethke, "Cuttings *(later)*")

## Closing

Help me, God of life,
in my struggle
to come alive.
Let me nourish the seeds
you plant in me,
and coax the delicate new shoots
toward the light,
where they can feed
on your warmth and radiance.

# Seeds: Dying and Rising

## Opening

God of mercy, there are times
when my life falls apart
and chaos surrounds me.
Is this brokenness
truly necessary for new meaning,
new ways of growing?
Does the husk of my existence need to be split
   open
in order for me to be reborn?

## Reading

Unless a wheat grain falls into the earth and dies,
it remains only a single grain;
but if it dies,
it yields a rich harvest.

(John 12:24)

## Reflection

A seed is lovingly planted in well-prepared ground,
a special seed, hard-kerneled and brown. The dark
soil encourages growth and color, and the seed
begins to turn from dark brown to green. The
outer husk cracks completely and becomes nourishment for fresh, new life. A tiny green shoot
slowly creeps out of the broken kernel and reaches
into the soil above. Slowly the roots sink deep,

taking hold of the dark earth. A tender shoot
breaks through grains of soil into the radiance of
warm light.

## Hymn

Whisper of running streams, and winter lightning.
The wild thyme unseen and the wild strawberry,
The laughter in the garden, echoed ecstasy
Not lost, but requiring, pointing to the agony
Of death and birth.

(T. S. Eliot, *Four Quartets*)

## Closing

The hardest thing,
God of patience and love,
is the waiting,
letting mysterious resources take over
and make new life out of seeming death.
I am never quite sure what I am waiting for.
In winter it is difficult to imagine life
rising from the cold earth.
Yet the gardener learns to wait patiently,
trusting the process that occurs
hidden in the darkness.

# Brother Sun

## Opening

Praised be You, my Lord, with all your creatures,
especially Sir Brother Sun,
Who is the day and through whom You give us
    light.
And he is beautiful and radiant with great
    splendor;
and bears a likeness of You, Most High One.

(Francis of Assisi,<br>"The Canticle of Brother Sun")

## Reading

Pride of the heights, a clear vault of the sky—
such is the beauty of the heavens, a glorious sight.
The sun, as he emerges, proclaims at his rising,
"How wonderful a thing, the work of the Most
    High!"

(Ecclesiasticus 43:1–2)

## Reflection

While I work in the garden the gently beneficent
sun spills over my shoulder and onto the earth,
imparting light and warmth, growth and fertility.
I think of the dark, passive earth dazzled by this
stream of glory. Scooping a fistful of soil, I feel the
warmth of penetrating light. If the sun can enter
this dark clod, then it can fill my murky heart,
uncover the hidden places, and scatter my doubt

and anxiety. Who would choose to stay in the shadows knowing that sunlight can penetrate and warm the dark places of the heart?

## Hymn

Sun, my relative
Be good coming out
Do something good for us.

Make me work,
So I can do anything in the garden
I hoe, I plant corn, I irrigate.

You, sun, be good going down at sunset
We lay down to sleep I want to feel good.

(Havasupai Indians, "A Prayer")

## Closing

Lord, you are my lover,
My longing,
My flowing stream,
My sun,
And I am your reflection.

(Mechtild of Magdeburg,
"How the Soul Speaks to God")

# Sister Moon

## Opening

Praised be You, my Lord, through Sister Moon and
the stars,
In heaven You formed them clear and precious
and beautiful.

(Francis of Assisi,
"The Canticle of Brother Sun")

## Reading

The day and the night are yours;
you fashioned the sun and the moon.
You established the bounds of the land;
summer and winter—you make them.

(Psalm 74:16–17)

## Reflection

The drama of a night sky: the tiny silver stars
blink and the moon hangs low, casting a shimmer-
ing blanket of light over the garden. Gardeners
who follow the "old ways" plant according to
moon phases: first and second quarters of the
moon for seeds that bear food aboveground, third
and fourth quarters of the moon for seeds that
bear food below the ground. In ancient times,
people believed that fruit trees planted under a
radiant new moon would produce abundant crops.
Of course, the moon's subtle power moves the
great ocean tides, and it's legendary influence
moves the hearts of women and men to love.

We are re-establishing our connection with the moon and, with it, our appreciation of the feminine wisdom of the earth's cycles of death and regeneration and the earth's groaning for unity and reconciliation. The light of the moon reminds us of fecundity, birth, earth wisdom, and that creation holds life in balance. In his meditation "Hagia Sophia," Thomas Merton writes of the invisible fecundity, the mysterious unity and integrity inherent in all things. He refers to this wordless, gently powerful presence as a mothering Wisdom, Hagia Sophia, and Mary, the mother of God. By making space in her body for God, Mary made space for the entire living world. Our Sister, Mary, gave birth to salvation, the healing of humanity, the bread and wine of life.

## Hymn

Watching the moon
at midnight,
solitary, mid-sky,
I knew myself completely,
no part left out.

(Izumi Shikibu, *The Ink Dark Moon*)

## Closing

God of wisdom, awaken me to the feminine voice that announces: "there is in all visible things an invisible fecundity, a dimmed light, a meek namelessness, a hidden wholeness," and let me be born again (Thomas Merton, "Hagia Sophia").

# Weather

## Opening

Awaken me
to your presence,
my Protector,
when storms
seem certain
with clouds blowing up
on a muggy afternoon.

## Reading

In the evening you say,
  "It will be fine; there's a red sky,"
and in the morning,
  "Stormy weather today; the sky is red and
    overcast."
You know how to read the face of the sky,
but you cannot read the signs of the times.

(Matthew 16:2–3)

## Reflection

The garden behind my house has been completely
ruined by the rains and storms of the last few days;
dark rivulets flow in every direction, stripping soil
away from roots, destroying new plantings. The
changing weather reminds me of the cycles of the
heart. We see ourselves tossed and turned by the
same old issues, good days follow bad. We hope
that some day we will discover solid ground so that
we are not so easily manipulated by the storm of

external events. Jesus surprises us. He tells us the Reign of God is now; we can find stability at the innermost depths of our being.

## Hymn

April brings
rain and melt,
warm water over gray drifts
of a dead land.
Early sun releases
creeks and streams;
water chatters day
and night
through gutters
and gardens.
Every spring
the gritty wind thrashes,
the rain wears dingy ruts
in our snowfields and
awakens a path
in our winter sleep.

## Closing

Help me weather
the storms of my life,
God, my protector,
and find refuge
in a secret center
where I am
intimately united
not only with myself
but with others,
all others.

# *Soil*

## Opening

I scoop some soil into my hands,
look at it, smell it,
and imagine how plants receive nourishment
from moist loam.
What a mystery, creator God,
this dark earth,
one that I have forgotten!

## Reading

Listen, a sower went out to sow. As he sowed,
some seeds fell on the edge of the path, and the
birds came and ate them up. Others fell on patches
of rock where they found little soil and sprang up
at once, because there was no depth of earth; but
as soon as the sun came up they were scorched
and, not having any roots, they withered away.
. . . Others fell on rich soil and produced their
crop, some a hundredfold, some sixty, some thirty.
(Matthew 13:3–9)

## Reflection

Nothing happens unless a plant finds a home in
rich soil—no growth, no birth, no nurturing. Seed
on rocky ground dies; seed thrown carelessly on
uncultivated ground becomes scattered; seed left
unprotected is eaten by birds. A seed grows when
it feels the maternal pressure and pulse envelop it,

when it draws sustenance from the fertile darkness. We must believe that God can be found in
the familiar, warm darkness of the heart just as
in the darkness of the earth; only then can the
human spirit flourish.

## Hymn

As I kneel to put the seeds in
careful as stitching, I am in love.
You are the bed we all sleep on.
You are the food we eat, the food
we ate, the food we will become.
We are walking trees rooted in you.
    (Marge Piercy, "The Common Living Dirt")

## Closing

Let me sink deep in the dark, fertile ground,
become planted within it, breathe it,
receive nourishment from it.
Sustained by you, God of mystery,
let me uncover
the direction
of my life
and the pattern of my growth.

# Roots

## Opening

O nourishing God,
a seed needs
tiny delicate strands of root
to draw nourishment from the moist earth
that cradles and nourishes it.
May my life be deeply rooted in you.
Nourish me so that I can continue
to seek out possibilities
and realize the potential of my heart.

## Reading

The just flourish like a palm tree,
they grow tall as a cedar of Lebanon.
Planted as they are in the house of the Creator,
they flourish in the courts of our God,
bearing fruit in old age like trees full of sap—
vigorous, wide-spreading—

(Psalm 92:12–14)

## Reflection

The heart is center of our being where intellect
and will and feelings, mind and body, past and
future come together. When we discover that
spot where our life holds together, we discover
the heart. That is why I call the heart the taproot of the whole person. When we grasp the
taproot of a dandelion to be pulled, or of a dog-
wood tree to be transplanted, we know that we
have taken hold of the whole plant. And there are

moments when something touched that very root
of our being. It went to our heart.

(David Steindl-Rast,
*Gratefulness, the Heart of Prayer*)

## Hymn

People who complain of loneliness must have lost
    something,
lost some living connection with the cosmos,
    out of themselves,
lost their life-flow
like a plant whose roots are cut.
And they are crying like plants whose roots are cut.
But the presence of other people will not give
    them new, rooted connection
it will only make them forget.
The thing to do is in solitude slowly and painfully
    put
forth new roots
into the unknown, and take root by oneself.

(D. H. Lawrence, "The Uprooted")

## Closing

Holy God,
help me see beyond
the outer crust,
so that I do not become trapped
by external forces,
confused,
not trusting
completely
the taproot
that draws hidden life
within.

# Fertilizing

## Opening

God of love and compassion,
I begin a compost pile
so that I can enrich
vegetables and perennials.
Give me the insight to see
that the heart
needs the decay of suffering
in order to bear the fruit of love.

## Reading

A man had a fig tree planted in his vineyard, and
he came looking for fruit on it but found none. He
said to his vinedresser, "For three years now I have
been coming to look for fruit on this fig tree and
finding none. Cut it down: why should it be taking
up the ground?" "Sir," the man replied, "leave it
one more year and give me time to dig round it
and manure it: it may bear fruit next year; if not,
then you can cut it down."

(Luke 13:6–9)

## Reflection

One lesson we learn from nature is that plants
do not grow unless they are fertilized. This is the
reason for composting and fertilizing. The same
law applies to human nature: suffering and awareness of the dark side of the self fertilizes our soul
so that it can bear the fruit of inner life. If we
experienced only prosperity we would not learn
how to love; compassion is fired in the crucible of
failure, loss, and suffering.

## Hymn

Behold this compost! behold it well!
Perhaps every mite has once form'd part of a sick
                              person—yet behold!
The grass of spring covers the prairies,
The bean bursts noiselessly through the mould
                              in the garden,
The delicate spear of the onion pierces upward,
The apple-buds cluster together on the
    apple-branches.
                    (Walt Whitman, "This Compost")

## Closing

Loving God,
give me the strength
to bear my suffering,
to face my shadow self,
so that my heart can be transformed,
and in turn
transform the hearts of others.

# Weeding

## Opening

God of earth and sky,
I bend down,
knees in the dirt,
to pull some weeds.
I feel their rubbery strength
as I tug,
their stubborn rootedness,
the spray of earth against my chest
as they suddenly come loose.
I recall the parts of my life that are a source
    of frustration, guilt, discomfort,
        and embarrassment.

## Reading

The kingdom of heaven may be compared to a
man who sowed good seed in his field; but while
men were sleeping, his enemy came and sowed
weeds among the wheat, and went away. So when
the plants came up and bore grain, then the weeds
appeared also. And the servants of the household-
er came and said to him, "Sir, did you not sow
good seed in your field? How then has it weeds?"
He said to them, "An enemy has done this." The
servants said to him, "Then do you want us to
go and gather them?" But he said, "No; lest in
gathering the weeds you root up the wheat along
with them."

(Adapted from Matthew 13:24–29)

## Reflection

One can never in this life be wholly free from such mishaps. But because some weeds happen among the corn, one should not for that reason throw away the good corn. Indeed, if it were well with a man and he knew himself well with God, all such sorrows and mishaps would turn into his great profit. For to good men all things come to good, . . . "Yes, even sins."

(Edmund Colledge and Bernard McGinn, trans.,
*Meister Eckhart*)

## Hymn

It is necessary that I rip stubborn tendrils
from this fertile, moist bed,
that I sink toward the ground
with each deliberate pull.

A breeze caresses my shoulders
curves around my cheek,
crumbled soil spills everywhere.
Gathered weeds wither in the heat.

I survey the ground, identify the intruders.
May they continue to appear,
a sign of the heart's disorder
to help us grow and love.

## Closing

Weeds, weeds, disorder—
all the unwelcome chaos, my God.
But this teaches me patience
and trust
in the constant ground of your love.

# Hoeing

## Opening

Help me, God, give me strength!
Hoeing is not easy!
An inner voice cries out
in rebellion for something less difficult.
Why should my hands grow rough,
my lips chap,
my back ache,
and my disposition turn irritable?
Are you breaking
the hardness of my heart
into fragments?

## Reading

Our hymn of praise belongs to you,
O God . . .
Thus have you prepared the land:
drenching its furrows,
breaking up its clods,
softening it with showers,
blessing its yield.

(Psalm 65:1,10)

## Reflection

Hoeing is tedious work that involves going one step
at a time while making your way down each row,
feeling the company of plants and getting to know
their condition firsthand. You work rocky stretches
of ground, soil hard and dry, thin and loose, or soft
humus, moist and rich. You become familiar with

all the hard-packed clay as well as the workable
ground. Above all, you learn to apply the energy of
your heart to this work, even though the task is
laborious and the results not immediately evident.

## Hymn

We go in withering July
To ply the hard incessant hoe;
Panting beneath the brazen sky
We sweat and grumble, but we go.

. . . . . . . . . . . . .

The sense that we have brought to birth
Out of the cold and heavy soil,
These blessed fruits and flowers of earth
Is large reward for all our toil.
                    (Ruth Pitter, "The Diehards")

## Closing

Hoeing teaches the heart
a simple language.
Attending to each plant
in turn,
lifting the soil,
wiping drops of sweat
from my eyes.
Working,
I discover a humble rhythm,
connection to the earth,
healing for my soul.
Prepare the ground of my heart
in your own way
and in your own time, Holy Wisdom,
and give me the strength
to participate.

# Watering

## Opening

Gracious God,
I love to watch the rain dance on the earth
and caress the leaves.
This silent act of rain is a pure gift,
but I never thought about it.
Yet how often I enjoyed the freshness of morning
  dew,
the smell of wet humus, the mirror wet
of glistening stone,
and the small rivulets that trace a path through
  my garden.

## Reading

For I shall pour out water
on the thirsty soil
and streams on the dry ground.

(Isaiah 44:3)

## Reflection

It seems to me that the garden can be watered in
four ways: by taking water from a well, which costs
us great labor; or by a waterwheel and buckets.
. . . (I have sometimes drawn it in this way: it
is less laborious than the other and gives more
water); or by a stream or a brook, which waters
the ground much better, for it saturates it more
thoroughly, and there is less need to water it often

44

. . . ; or by heavy rain, when the Lord waters it
with no labor of ours, a way incomparably better
than any of those which have been described.
   (Teresa of Ávila, in *Thomas Merton on Mysticism*)

## Hymn

After a night of rain
this garden so
fragile it's never raked, but swept,
lies on a bed
soft as itself, and all the morning, fed
by the rain banked richly below,
bathes in a glow
gentle as candle-light.
   (Brad Leithauser, "In a Japanese Moss Garden")

## Closing

Good Jesus, the water of your teaching
flows in silence. . . .
Your voice never strains nor shouts.
You do not force us to hear you.
You ask only
that we open
our hearts to you,
and
in tranquillity
your love enters our souls.

(Aelred of Rievaulx,
"The Water of Your Teaching")

# *Pruning*

## Opening

God, my wise gardener,
prune the dead and diseased
parts of my life
so that I can come alive
in a new way.

## Reading

I am the vine.
The Creator is the vinedresser.
Those branches of mine
that do not bear any fruit,
the Vinedresser cuts off.
The branches that were heavy with fruit,
the Creator prunes carefully,
so that they will bear even more fruit.

(Adapted from John 15:1–2)

## Reflection

At first it seems that pruning stops further growth,
but if done properly, it can guide a plant's growth
and induce it to flourish. By affecting the inner
being of a plant, pruning lets the sap run more
directly. Fruitless branches can drain away the life
of a plant, just like old angers, greed, and a selfish
spirit sap away our life. Pruning, though seemingly
violent and harmful, can actually restore plants to
greening fruitfulness.

## Hymn

Meeting with Time, slack thing, said I,
Thy Scythe is dull; whet it for shame.
No marvel Sir, he did reply,
If it at length deserve some blame:
But where one man would have me grind it,
Twenty for one too sharp do find it.

Perhaps some such of old did pass,
Who above all things loved this life;
To whom thy scythe a hatchet was,
Which now is but a pruning-knife.
Christ's coming hath made man thy debtor,
Since by thy cutting he grows better.

(George Herbert, "Time")

## Closing

Holy Wisdom,
do not let me forget
that I need to make choices
and say
no
to those things that
hinder
my growth.
Give me faith
in the spirit's strength
to revive itself
and lead me to a new life.

# *Flowers*

## Opening

We were enclosed,
O eternal Father,
Within the garden of your breast.
You drew us out of your holy mind
like a flower.

(Catherine of Siena, *Prayers*)

## Reading

For see, winter is past,
the rains are over and gone.
Flowers are appearing on the earth.
The season of glad songs has come.

(Song of Songs 2:11–12)

## Reflection

What form expresses the abundance of love better
than a flower? Flowers ripen and blossom, pulse
with loving energy. They are revelations of grace
uncurling like the hands of a child, invitations to
beauty and freedom.

It is easy to see how the flower could symbolize
new life, the unfolding consciousness of a unified,
harmonious self. The rose represents Christ, the
thousand-petaled lotus, the "One." Flowers remind
us that our lives are nothing more than the blossoming of love. We are invariably drawn back to

this realization when we walk among flowers and rediscover their romantic forms, their bold colors and heady scents. Even when the flowers are gone we sit and think about them. Why? Because they recall the innocence and nostalgia of a forgotten love.

## Hymn

These are thy wonders, Lord of love,
To make us see we are but flowers that glide:
Which when we once can find and prove,
Thou hast a garden for us, where to bide.

(George Herbert, "The Flower")

## Closing

Lord, you are like a wild flower. You spring up in places where we least expect you. The bright colour of your grace dazzles us. When we reach down to pluck you, hoping to possess you for our own, you blow away in the wind. And if we tried to destroy you, by stamping on you and kicking you, you would come back to life. Lord, may we come to expect you anywhere and everywhere. May we rejoice in your beauty. Far from trying to possess you, may you possess us.

(Henry Suso, "Like a Wild Flower")

# *Always the Rose*

## Opening

Wherever they are found,
loving God,
let roses,
seductive and breathtakingly beautiful,
bring happiness.
May they grace
every corner of the heart.

## Reading

Listen, my devoted children.
Blossom just like the rose
that flourishes by the spring.
Scent the breeze with your fragrance
like sweet incense,
and flower like the lilies.
Sing praise to the Creator
for the wonders of the earth.

(Adapted from Ecclesiasticus 39:13–14)

## Reflection

Roses in the afternoon light, their petals in shades
of salmon, crimson, and gold, fill the landscape
with color and warmth. The important thing is
not to merely look at a rose, but to let yourself

become absorbed in its color and shape until it takes form within you. Gaze at its exquisite center, and let it become music that draws you inward. Become the rose completely. It will invite you to unfold and blossom without restriction. All your cares may be forgotten, at least for a while, and you will "sing praise to the Creator."

## Hymn

The richness at the center of a rose
is the richness of your heart.
Unfurl it as she does:
her girded boundary is all your affliction.

Set her free in song
or in great love.
Do not shield the rose:
she would burn you with her brilliance!

(Gabriela Mistral, "The Rose")

## Closing

Gracious God,
let my life blossom like the rose,
in concert with eternal music,
flowing toward you
in love and faith.

# Vegetable Garden

## Opening

All-good God, thank you
for vegetable gardens.
They are not only productive and useful,
ordered and satisfying,
but even beautiful—
the gentle green plot,
deep and soft,
nestling a world
of dramatic forms.

## Reading

Build houses, settle down;
plant gardens and eat what they produce.

(Jeremiah 29:5)

## Reflection

If our only reason for growing vegetables is to save
money, we may be disheartened to find that the
difference between homegrown produce and store-
bought is very slight. But what if we refuse to put
a monetary value on the garden and simply take
delight in it? We should let vegetable gardening
bring us into an intimate relationship with the
earth and introduce us to lettuce, beans, and carrots as surprising shapes that can transform our
vision.

## Hymn

Tomatoes,
the essence of summer growth,
thick, ripe,
reeking of moist
earth and sun,
absorbing water
like a desert dweller.
Just take a look
at these,
all healthy,
fat off the vine,
the crimson joy
of summer's offspring.

## Closing

God of the harvest,
I celebrate the earthiness
of potatoes
just dug up,
the sweetness of peas,
white flowers on early beans,
beads of dew
on bulging tomatoes,
sugar snap peas,
runner beans,
young carrots,
and a vegetable garden
full of flowers
attracting bees and butterflies.

# A Passion for Herbs

## Opening

God, you who secure my soul,
may these herbs protect me
as they protected Jonah;
may they calm my troubled heart
and keep my spirit buoyant,
ready to celebrate your nearness.

## Reading

God then ordained that a castor-oil plant should
grow up over Jonah to give shade for his head and
soothe his ill-humor; Jonah was delighted with the
castor-oil plant.

(Jonah 4:6)

## Reflection

Anyone who walks through an herb garden and
lingers among sweet thyme, spicy basil, the sharp
bergamot and mint, the familiar dill and anise,
takes away a memory of scents that wafts through
the mind, bringing it contentment and peace for
many hours.

Herbs are a joy! They offer pleasures that are
sensual, creative, and healthy. They can free the
senses and calm the anxious spirit. We spend most
of our time dealing with practical affairs and
attempting to control our life. Growing herbs,
tasting them, and smelling them gives us the
opportunity to discover the spiritual, sensuous

life—to reclaim our humanness. Creating a meal with herbs fresh from the garden is truly the harvest of a gifted life.

## Hymn

I know a bank where the wild thyme blows,
Where oxlips and the nodding violet grows,
Quite overcanopied with luscious woodbine,
With sweet muskroses, and with eglantine.

(William Shakespeare,
"A Midsummer Night's Dream")

## Closing

Creator of all life,
let the fragrant herbs be signs
of your goodness and beauty
touching my life in an intimate way.
Let them expand my senses
and give me health,
so that I can appreciate your nearness
in the world around me.

# Butterflies

## Opening

Butterflies blown by the soft breeze
float through the garden,
settle on a red geranium, and raise
their soft dotted wings
in an arch—
another breeze and they are gone.
God of freedom,
you created my soul
so that it could grow toward maturity
and fly free in your love.

## Reading

The Creator formed the human being from the
soil and then breathed life into the human's nos-
trils. The human being came to life.

(Adapted from Genesis 2:7)

## Reflection

Traditionally the butterfly is a symbol of the resurrected human soul. The life cycle of caterpillar,
chrysalis, and butterfly symbolizes life, death, and
resurrection. Teresa of Ávila used this image to
refer to a stage of prayer in which persons, having
been released from attachments, are able to fly

free and do what they are created to do. When the soul finds freedom from restrictions, if only for a brief time, it suddenly recognizes its deep desire to praise God; the chrysalis cracks and releases a beautiful butterfly with shining wings.

## Hymn

It is blue-butterfly day here in spring,
And with these sky-flakes down in flurry on flurry
There is more unmixed color on the wing
Than flowers will show for days unless they hurry.

But these are flowers that fly and all but sing:
And now from having ridden out desire
They lie closed over in the wind and cling
Where wheels have freshly sliced the April mire.

(Robert Frost, "Blue-Butterfly Day")

## Closing

God who offers revelation
in unexpected ways,
may the beautiful image of a butterfly
call my soul back
to a loving relationship with you.

# The Earthworm

## Opening

God of the universe,
you who cherishes all life,
teach me not to take any creature,
no matter how small or insignificant,
for granted.

## Reading

The creeping things of earth will give you lessons.
(Job 12:8)

## Reflection

Even the small earthworm that winds its way
through the dark earth, creating caverns, has
beauty and meaning for the gardener. Earthworms
break down decomposable matter into fine humus
and aerate the soil, so their presence signals rich
earth. The gardener mulches to encourage earthworms because of their enormous value in the
garden. Saint Francis of Assisi showed great tenderness for the small earthworm, picking up any
he found in the path and placing them where trav-
elers could not tread on them. The earthworm
reminds us of the humility necessary for all inner
work. We enrich our heart in small, hidden ways.

# Hymn

Who really respects the earthworm,
the farmworker far under the grass in the soil.
He keeps the earth always changing.
He works entirely full of soil,
speechless with soil, and blind.

He is the underneath farmer, the underground
    one,
where the fields are getting on their harvest
    clothes.
Who really respects him,
this deep and calm earth-worker,
this deathless, gray, tiny farmer in the planet's soil.

(Harry Martinson, "The Earthworm,"
Robert Bly, trans.)

# Closing

God of the weak and unprotected,
the small earthworm
makes me consider
how much you must love me,
and how much I am responsible
to give my life humbly to others.

# Trees

## Opening

What magnificent creations, God of wonder!
They grow from generation to generation
providing sanctuary
for songbirds, owls, and insects.
We rest against them
—cedar, pine, oak, sycamore—
and find comfort and healing
under their branches.

## Reading

I know: a cedar tree in the Lebanon
with noble branches, dense foliage, lofty height.
Its top pierces the clouds.
The waters have made it grow, the deep has made
    it tall,
pouring its rivers round the place where it is
    planted,
sending rivulets to all the wild trees.

. . . . . . . . . . . . . . . .

I had made it so lovely with its many branches
that it was the envy of every tree in Eden, in the
    garden of God.

(Ezekiel 31:3–9)

# Reflection

The soul in the body is like sap in a tree, and the
soul's powers are like the form of the tree. How?
The intellect in the soul is like the greenery of the
tree's branches and leaves, the will like its flowers,
the mind like its bursting firstfruits, the reason like
the perfected mature fruit, and the senses like its
size and shape.

(Hildegard of Bingen, *Scivias*)

# Hymn

Elm, laburnum, hawthorn, oak:
all the incredible leaves expand
on their dusty branches, like
Japanese paper flowers in water,
like anything one hardly believes
will really work this time; and
I am a stupefied spectator
as usual. . . .

(Fleur Adcock, "Trees")

# Closing

O eternal Godhead!
What a wonder,
in your light,
to see your creature as a pure tree,
a tree you drew out of yourself,

.    .    .    .    .    .    .    .    .    .

You planted it and fused it
into the humanity you had formed
from the earth's clay.

(Catherine of Siena, *Prayers*)

# Apple Trees

## Opening

God of power and might,
who formed all living things,
I gaze at an ancient apple tree,
its gnarled limbs
twisting toward the sun,
and I wonder at the stories
it holds in its branches,
the ripe fruit it has produced through the years.

## Reading

There is no sound tree that produces rotten fruit,
nor again a rotten tree that produces sound fruit.
Every tree can be told by its own fruit.

(Luke 6:43–44)

## Reflection

Apples are delicious, attractive, seductive, a true
temptation for the soul and body. The blossoms of
trees are a delight to bees, and the nectar produces
a light amber honey. Children love climbing the
branches of apple trees and savoring the sweet
juice. It is easy to imagine that apples are the rich
bounty of a healthy tree, the fruit of life. Even
bruised apples, rejected by many, have an over-
powering sweetness and make wonderful apple-
sauce and cider. They remind us of an inherent
goodness in our life even in times of pain and
difficulty.

# Hymn

Toward the gardens,
Toward the orchards,
   I am going.
If you want to stay here,
Stay here—
   I am going!

.   .   .   .   .   .

The smell of apples arises
   from the orchard of my soul.
One whiff and I am gone—
   Toward a feast of apples
   I am going.

           (Rumi, "The Body Is Too Slow for Me")

# Closing

Creator of abundant sensations,
let the sweetness of apples
remind me of the goodness
in the depths of my own being,
the sweet juice that fills my soul
when my heart stores goodness.

# *Along Garden Paths*

## Opening

This winding garden path
coaxes me along,
just as you do, my wise Guide.
I stop and gaze at roses,
smell the herbs,
then move onward,
forgetting my concerns.

## Reading

I shall guide them to streams of water,
by a smooth path
where they will not stumble.

(Jeremiah 31:9)


In verdant pastures you give me repose.
Beside restful waters you lead me;
you refresh my soul.
You guide me in right paths
for your name's sake.

(Psalm 23:2–3)

## Reflection

A garden is a wilderness until there is a path
through it. A path provides a perspective so that
the onlooker can discover beauty of color and
form. Paths also pull us along. They meander,
providing curves, slopes, and corners that track
the garden landscape as well as the gardener's
spirit. When the path is walked many times, it
tends to become etched in the heart as well as on
the feet. Without realizing it, the gardener uncov-
ers not only an external route but also a soul-path.
The path becomes a way of prayer, a communion
of spirit with Spirit under the spell of beauty.

## Hymn

Smooth, simple path! whose undulating line,
With sidelong tufts of flowery fragrance crowned,
'Plain, in its neatness', spans my garden ground;
What, though two acres thy brief course confine,
Yet sun and shade, and hill and dale are thine.
                    (Erasmus Darwin, "To a Gravel Walk")

## Closing

God, my constant companion
during good times and bad,
lead me along the paths
that refresh my heart
and nourish my exhausted spirit.
I may often feel lost,
but I turn to you,
my steady guide,
who shows me the way of truth.

# A Place of Rest

## Opening

O Lord God, give us peace,
for you have given all things to us,
the peace of rest,
the peace of the sabbath,
the peace without an evening.

(Saint Augustine, *Confessions*)

## Reading

On the seventh day, God finished creating the heavens and the earth. So the Creator rested from the holy labor, deciding to make the seventh day blessed, a day of rest and re-creation. God rested, creation could rest, too.

(Adapted from Genesis 2:2–3)

## Reflection

Resting in the garden reminds us to simplify our life and listen to inner music. Remaining there allows our heart to expand; we discover new sensations, and life takes on a different texture. We may find a preferred spot, a secret corner to sit quietly and pray, reflect, or sink into the silence. Once in this garden, we anchor ourselves in the here and now, not in some future dream. Time stops, and we are suddenly happy in the present moment.

## Hymn

Here at the fountain's sliding foot,
Or at some fruit-tree's mossy root,
Casting the body's vest aside,
My soul into the boughs does glide:
There like a bird it sits, and sings,
Then whets, and combs its silver wings;
And, till prepared for longer flight,
Waves in its plumes the various light.

(Andrew Marvell, "The Garden")

## Closing

It's time to rest, holy God.
I have had enough activity.
Teach me to attend to each moment,
to realize that the world's business
will not offer solace,
or help me to say yes
to the stillness
at the center of my being.
Let me share the solitude I find in the garden
with others
in a way that is loving and free.

# Night Chant

## Opening

Thank you, God,
for your love and protection
throughout this day,
and for this night solitude.
I offer you my life,
continue to transform it
during these hours of quiet and rest.

## Reading

O God, you are my God whom I eagerly seek;
for you my flesh longs and my soul thirsts
like the earth, parched, lifeless, and without water.

. . . . . . . . . . . . . . .

On my bed I will remember you,
and through the night watches I will meditate on
    you:
because you are my help,
and in the shadow of your wings I shout for joy.

(Psalm 63:1–7)

## Reflection

In the evening I visit the garden alone. The breeze,
cool and soft, and an aroma of flowers fill the air.
Remaining without care, forgetting plants, and

letting my life fall silent, I stand with my heart
open, releasing all that I have clung to through the
day. In the evening the garden becomes a retreat
filled with pungent scents lost in the daytime heat,
and unimagined forms and textures of bushes,
leaves, and bark. As shapes fade into the shadows,
my heart expands beyond the usual boundaries.
I wait for tenderness along the dark slopes of
the landscape and, among the waves of silence,
I listen.

## Hymn

My soul, there is a country
  Far beyond the stars,

. . . . . . . .

If thou canst get but thither,
  There grows the flower of peace,
The rose that cannot wither,
  Thy fortress, and thy ease.

                    (Henry Vaughan, "Peace")

## Closing

Thank you, loving God,
for allowing me to participate
in the gentle peace
that covers the earth
in this mysterious solitude.
Branches of trees
carry my dreams across the darkness,
and my heart settles secure in you.
You touch my heart best at night.

# The Fountain

## Opening

God of eternal life,
you say, "Come into the garden,
taste the refreshing springs
of truth!
Drink the water of life
at a place where the garden is most secret,
at the fountain of pure love."

## Reading

She is a garden enclosed,
my sister, my promised bride;
a garden enclosed,
a sealed fountain.

. . . . . . .

Fountain of the garden,
well of living water,
streams flowing down from Lebanon!

(Song of Songs 4:12–15)

## Reflection

Referring to the inner potential in each of our lives that rises unexpectedly into consciousness like a dream, Carl Jung writes: "The dreamer takes the plunge into the dark and discovers a beautiful garden in the depths, symmetrically laid out, with a fountain in the centre" (*Dreams*). Jung's interpretation of the dream? "The garden with the fountain are all one and the same thing: the self" (*Dreams*).

## Hymn

How well I know that flowing spring
    in black of night.

The eternal fountain is unseen.
How well I know where she has been
    in black of night.

I do not know her origin.
None. Yet in her all things begin
    in black of night.

(John of the Cross, "The Fountain")

## Closing

I beseech you, merciful God,
to allow me to drink from the stream
which flows from your fountain of life.
May I taste the sweet beauty of its waters,
which spring from the very depths of your truth.
(Columbanus, "The Fountain of Life")

# Vineyards

## Opening

God, you who renews
my heart's gladness,
lead me to the vineyards
where I can learn to celebrate
loving relationships
and the gift of my life.

## Reading

Come, my love,
let us go to the fields.
We will spend the night in the villages,
and in the early morning we will go to the
    vineyards.
We will see if the vines are budding,
if their blossoms are opening,
if the pomegranate trees are in flower.

(Song of Songs 7:12–13)

## Reflection

"Judah and Israel dwell in safety, all people resting
under their vines and their fig trees" (adapted
from 1 Kings 4:25). The vineyard represents a
foretaste of the glory to come, a place of abundance and blessing. Vines budding or blossoming
and plump grapes ready to pick are symbols of the
land of Israel and signify happiness, peace, and
security for all.

## Hymn

O brother, bring the pure wine
   of love and freedom.

But master, a tornado is coming.

More wine!—
   we will teach this storm
   a thing or two about whirling!

(Rumi, "Divine Intoxication")

## Closing

Jesus, you identified yourself
with the vine,
offering paradise
to all who would drink
the pure wine of love and freedom.
Liberate my soul,
and fill me with love.

# Garden of Love

## Opening

Breathe into the garden of my soul,
Spirit of Life,
and intensify my desire to love,
even though it may be accompanied
not only with joy,
but incredible suffering.

## Reading

Beloved: Awake, north wind,
    come, wind of the south!
    Breathe over my garden,
    to spread its sweet smell around.
    Let my love come into his garden,
    let him taste its most exquisite fruits.

Lover: I come into my garden,
    my sister, my promised bride,
    I pick my myrrh and balsam,
    I eat my honey and my honeycomb,
    I drink my wine and my milk.

(Song of Songs 4:16; 5:1)

## Reflection

The south wind is a delightful breeze: it causes
rain, makes the herbs and plants germinate, opens
the flowers, and scatters their fragrance. Its effects
are the opposite of those of the north wind. The

soul, by this breeze, refers to the Holy Spirit, who awakens love. When this divine breeze strikes her, it wholly enkindles and refreshes her.

(John of the Cross, Collected Works)

## Hymn

Where did your lover go,
O loveliest of women?
Which way did your lover turn
so that we can help you seek him?

My love went down to his garden,
to the beds of spices,
to pasture his flock on the grass
and gather lilies.
I belong to my love, and my love to me.

(Song of Songs 6:1–2)

## Closing

In whatever direction I turn
I find unutterable love.
So we can never be excused for not loving you,

· · · · · · · · · · · · · ·

for I did not exist
and you made me.
Whatever I want to love,
whatever has being,
I find in you—

(Catherine of Siena, Prayers)

# Harvesting

## Opening

The air is crisp,
the trees are ablaze in gold and orange,
and gardens lean under the weight.
Bountiful God,
while harvesting ripe vegetables and blossoms,
my attention turns to the fullness
of life,
the richness
of the bounty,
and the connectedness of all things.

## Reading

May those who sow in tears
reap with songs of joy!
Those that go forth weeping,
carrying the seed for sowing,
shall come home with shouts of joy,
bringing the sheaves with them.

(Psalm 126:5–6)

## Reflection

Ultimately, there came a day when the garden was
groaning with its own bounty. (For weeks, everything seemed to be happening so slowly; now it
was happening amazingly fast.) Now each trip
meant I would fill my green rubber bucket with
wonderful ripe things: flaming peppers, tomatoes,
vibrant green lettuce, parsley, cucumbers. I loved

cutting the vegetables from their stems, releasing
them from their green tethers and putting them
into my bucket, hearing the plop as they hit the
bottom. And to pluck a huge tomato with the
merest touch, hold it, weighty and juicy, in my
hands—that act carried me the whole morning.
I was so full of contentment then. Resolution was
everywhere.

(Richard Goodman, French Dirt)

## Hymn

Summer ends now; now, barbarous in beauty, the
    stooks arise
  Around; up above, what wind-walks! what love-
    ly behaviour
Of silk-sack clouds! has wilder, wilful-wavier
Meal-drift moulded ever and melted across skies?

(Gerard Manley Hopkins,<br>"Hurrahing in Harvest")

## Closing

With gratitude,
bountiful God,
I gather berries,
pick apples,
and retrieve the last of the vegetables
from the garden.
Thank you
for autumn smells
of bonfires,
rotting leaves,
and newly turned earth!

# Blessings

## Opening

Bless the Creator, all plants that flourish greenly.
Give praise! Glory in the one who made you!

(Adapted from Daniel 3:74)

## Reading

Then the angel showed me the river of life, rising
from the throne of God and of the Lamb and
flowing crystal-clear. Down the middle of the city
street, on either bank of the river were the trees of
life, which bear twelve crops of fruit in a year, one
in each month, and the leaves of which are the
cure for the nations.

(Revelations 22:1–2)

## Reflection

Is it possible, Lord, for a soul which has received
such blessings as you have bestowed on my soul,
still to remain so hard and stubborn? Yes, I know
it is possible, because I so frequently rebuff your
advances and reject your blessings. . . .

Teach me, Lord, to sing of your mercies. Turn
my soul into a garden, where the flowers dance in
the gentle breeze, praising you with their beauty.

(Teresa of Ávila, "A Garden of Flowers")

## Hymn

the green of Jesus
is breaking the ground
and the sweet
smell of delicious Jesus
is opening the house and
the dance of Jesus music
has hold of the air and
the world is turning
in the body of Jesus and
the future is possible

> (Lucille Clifton, "spring song")

## Closing

i thank You God for most this amazing
day:for the leaping greenly spirits of trees
and a blue true dream of sky;and for everything
which is natural which is infinite which is yes

> (e. e. cummings, "i thank You God
> for most this amazing")

# Measureless Light

## Opening

You, all-accomplishing
Word of the Father,
are the light of primordial
daybreak over the spheres.
You, the foreknowing
mind of divinity,
foresaw all your works
as you willed them,
your prescience hidden
in the heart of your power,
your power like a wheel around the world,
whose circling never began
and never slides to an end.
     (Hildegard of Bingen, "Song to the Creator")

## Reading

God, who alone is immortal,
whose home is in inaccessible light,
whom no human being has seen
or is able to see.

     (1 Timothy 6:16)

## Reflection

This early evening walk around the garden is
dreamlike. A gentle, soft light bathes the leaves
and blossoms, and cascades around the trees. It
makes me feel touched by mystery, renewed,
graced. It is a time not to think, but to taste the

air and gaze out beyond the usual boundaries, to
imagine something beyond the tame world I have
accepted.

## Hymn

Light traveled over the wide field;
Stayed.
The weeds stopped swinging.
The mind moved, not alone,
Through the clear air, in the silence.

> Was it light?
> Was it light within?
> Was it light within light?
> Stillness becoming alive,
> Yet still?

(Theodore Roethke, "The Lost Son")

## Closing

O light-giving light
in whose light we see light!
In your light I see
and without it I cannot see,

. . . . . . . . .

In your light we come to know
that you are this matchless eternal garden,
and you hold enclosed within yourself
both the flowers and the fruits—

(Catherine of Siena, *Prayers*)

# God's Garden

## Opening

God of love,
you call me
and break my hold on life,
opening up distant horizons,
inviting me into a garden
that has no boundaries.

## Reading

I did the planting,
Apollos did the watering,
but God
gave growth.
In this,
neither the planter nor the waterer
counts for anything;
only God,
who gives growth.

(1 Corinthians 3:6–7)

## Reflection

At times when we experience the deepest love, we
find ourselves in an infinitely vast garden, God's
garden. God draws us into the center of our being
and reveals a garden of divine beauty. When we
answer the invitation "Come enter my garden," we
are rewarded with joy and a banquet of love. The
fullness of this love overflows into daily life and
inspires us to serve others. Through the awareness

of this love we realize that the inner garden is not
our own, but God's, a place where God wanders
and takes delight.

## Hymn

I am the one whose praise
echoes on high.

I adorn all the earth.

I am the breeze
that nurtures all things
green.
I encourage blossoms to flourish with ripening
    fruits.
I am led by the spirit to feed
the purest streams.

I am the rain
coming from the dew
that causes the grasses to laugh
with the joy of life.

(Hildegard of Bingen, *Meditations*)

## Closing

What a joy it is,
Gardener of love and happiness,
to discover you
at home
in my soul!

# Desert Garden

## Opening

Even if the fig tree refuses to blossom,
the vines yield no fruit,
the olive crop disappoints
and the fields yield no food;
I shall rejoice in you, God of the wilderness.

(Adapted from Habakkuk 3:17–18)

## Reading

Yahweh will always guide you,
will satisfy your needs
in the scorched land;
[Yahweh] will give strength to your bones
and you will be like a watered garden,
like a flowing spring
whose waters never run dry.

(Isaiah 58:11)

## Reflection

What if your heart feels like a desert wilderness:
no oasis, no rock formations, only a dry, desolate
landscape of endless waves of sand? Growth seems
impossible, and remaining in the desert and waiting, having faith that barren terrain will one day

flourish, appears to be a waste of time. Yet anyone who witnesses the desert after a spring rain sees wildflowers miraculously appearing out of nowhere; golden poppies and purple owlclover blooms fill the wasteland. If, like Ezekiel, we find ourselves in a valley full of bones, should we not recall Isaiah's vision of a wilderness that blossoms like a rose?

## Hymn

Don't say, don't say there is no water
to solace the dryness at our hearts.
I have seen

the fountain springing out of the rock wall
and you drinking there. And I too
before your eyes

found footholds and climbed
to drink the cool water.

> (Denise Levertov, "The Fountain")

## Closing

Let the desert and the dry lands
be glad,
let the wasteland rejoice and bloom;
like the asphodel, let it burst into flower,
let it rejoice and sing for joy.

> (Isaiah 35:1–2)

# Garden of Sorrows

## Opening

Jesus, you have given us hope, because you
endured all the spiritual and physical hardships
which mortal nature can suffer. In Gethsemane
your soul was in torment, and your heart shook
at the prospect of the physical pain to come.

(Saint Bonaventura, *Book of Prayers*)

## Reading

Then Jesus came with them to a plot of land
called Gethsemane; and he said to his disciples,
"Stay here while I go over there to pray." He took
Peter and the two sons of Zebedee with him. And
he began to feel sadness and anguish.

   Then he said to them, "My soul is sorrowful to
the point of death. Wait here and stay awake with
me."

(Matthew 26:36–38)

## Reflection

The gardener helps Christ carry the cross and
reflects that the Lord lived with it all during His
life.

(Teresa of Ávila, *Collected Works*)

## Hymn

I worked out anguish in a garden.
Without the flowers,
The shadow of trees on snow, their punctuation,
I might not have survived

. . . . . . . . .

Learned to clear myself as I have cleared the
    pasture,
Learned to wait,
Learned that change is always in the making.
                    (May Sarton, "Gestalt at Sixty")

## Closing

Jesus, let me remain with you
in this place of darkness;
calm my weary, fearful heart,
and open it to your love,
so that I may gain life
and learn to fulfill your will.

# Walking in Paradise

## Opening

Holy God,
help me cultivate
the virtues of faith, hope, and love
so that I can walk with you
in the garden of paradise
forever.

## Reading

"In truth I tell you, today you will be with me in paradise."

(Luke 23:43)

## Reflection

When monarchs bestowed a special honor on one of their subjects in ancient times, the person was chosen to walk in the ruler's garden as a special friend and companion of the monarch. Jesus promised the thief that he would walk with Christ in the garden of paradise, a place that the Jews believed the righteous would go after the Resurrection. Like the thief, we look forward to the promise of a time when Jesus will walk with us in the garden of our heart and find joy in our company.

# Hymn

"Remember me" implored the Thief!
Oh Hospitality!
My Guest "Today in Paradise"
I give thee guaranty.

That Courtesy will fair remain
When the Delight is Dust
With which we sight this mightiest case
Of compensated Trust.

Of all we are allowed to hope
But Affidavit stands
That this was due where most we fear
Be unexpected Friends.

(Emily Dickinson, *Complete Poems*)

# Closing

Ruler of my heart,
it is a delight
to spend time with you
in the garden,
to speak with you
and enjoy your friendship.
Transform my life
into a flowering garden
where I can always receive you.

# Eden

## Opening

Gracious God, lead me
into an Eden
where my life can be restored
into a garden of promise,
where you create
a new world for me.

## Reading

He will turn her desert into an Eden
and her wastelands
into the garden of Yahweh.
Joy and gladness will be found in her,
thanksgiving and the sound of music.

(Isaiah 51:3)

## Reflection

Lent had started and Easter was approaching.
I began to go for strolls in the fields. The world
had become a paradise; the snows of Olympus
sparkled in the sunlight while the fields below
shone bright green and the returning swallows,
like shuttles of a loom, wove spring into the air.
Small white and yellow wildflowers, pushing up
the soil with their tiny heads, began to emerge
into the sunlight in order to see the world above.
Someone must have rolled back the earthen tomb-
stones above them: they were being resurrected.

Someone? . . . Who? Doubtlessly God, God of
the innumerable faces: sometimes a flower, sometimes a bird or a fresh shoot on a grapevine, sometimes wheat.

(Nikos Kazantzakis, *Report to Greco*)

## Hymn

What wondrous life is this I lead!
Ripe apples drop about my head;
The luscious clusters of the vine
Upon my mouth do crush their wine;
The nectarine, and curious peach,
Into my hands themselves do reach;
Stumbling on melons, as I pass,
Ensnared with flowers, I fall on grass.

(Andrew Marvell, "The Garden")

## Closing

God of hope and love,
let me not remain
isolated from you
by trying to master
my own destiny.
Guide me toward your lush garden
of inexhaustible riches
and refreshing waters.

# Acknowledgments *(continued)*

The psalms in this book are from *Psalms Anew: In Inclusive Language*, compiled by Nancy Schreck and Maureen Leach (Winona, MN: Saint Mary's Press, 1986). Copyright © 1986 by Saint Mary's Press. All rights reserved.

The scriptural material cited as "adapted from" is freely adapted. These adaptations are not to be understood or used as official translations of the Bible.

All other scriptural quotations in this book are from the New Jerusalem Bible. Copyright © 1985 by Doubleday, a division of Bantam Doubleday Dell Publishing Group, New York, and Darton, Longman and Todd, London. Used with permission.

The quote on page 6 is from *Plant Dreaming Deep*, by May Sarton (New York: W. W. Norton and Company, 1968), page 119. Copyright © 1968 by May Sarton.

The excerpts on pages 8, 18–19, and 86 are from *The Collected Works of St. Teresa of Ávila*, volume 1, translated by Kieran Kavanaugh and Otilio Rodriguez (Washington, DC: ICS Publications, 1976), pages 137, 113, and 115, respectively. Copyright © 1976 by the Washington Province of Discalced Carmelites. Used with permission.

The excerpt on pages 10–11 is from *Second Nature: A Gardener's Education*, by Michael Pollan (New York: Dell Publishing, 1991), pages 143–144. Copyright © 1991 by Michael Pollan.

The excerpt from "Prayers and Sayings of the Mad Farmer" on page 11 is from *Farming: A Handbook*, by Wendell Berry. Copyright © 1969 by Wendell Berry. Reprinted by permission of Harcourt, Brace and Company.

The excerpts on pages 12, 48, 61, 75, and 81 are reprinted from *The Prayers of Catherine of Siena*, edited by Suzanne Noffke (New York: Paulist Press, 1983), pages 189, 147, 18, 186–187, and 187–188, respectively. Copyright © 1983 by Suzanne Noffke. Used by permission of Paulist Press.

The excerpts by Henry Vaughan on pages 15 and 69; the excerpts by George Herbert on pages 23, 47, and 49; and the excerpts by Andrew Marvell on pages 67 and 91 are from *Four Metaphysical Poets: An Anthology of Poetry by Donne, Herbert, Marvell and Vaughan*, edited by Richard Willmott (Cambridge, England: Cambridge University Press, 1985), pages 140–141 and 143; pages 91, 96, and 88; pages 115 and 114–115, respectively. Copyright © 1985 by Cambridge University Press.

The excerpt on pages 16–17 is from *The Secret Garden*, by Frances Hodgson Burnett (Boston: David R. Godine, 1987), page 80. Copyright © 1987 by David R. Godine.

The poem by Lauris Edmond on page 17 is from *New and Selected Poems* (Auckland: Oxford University Press, 1991). Reprinted by permission of the author.